AMERICA DEBATES™

AMERICA DEBATES GENETIC DNA TESTING

Elizabeth Boskey

rosen publishing's
**rosen
central**

New York

To both my families: the one I chose, and the one I was given

Published in 2008 by The Rosen Publishing Group, Inc.
29 East 21st Street, New York, NY 10010

Copyright © 2008 by The Rosen Publishing Group, Inc.

First Edition

Library of Congress Cataloging-in-Publication Data

Boskey, Elizabeth.
America debates genetic DNA testing / Elizabeth Boskey.—1st ed.
    p. cm.—(America debates)
Includes bibliographical references.
ISBN-13: 978-1-4042-1926-7
ISBN-10: 1-4042-1926-9
1. Genetic screening—Moral and ethical aspects. I. Title.
RB155.65.B67 2007
362.196'04207—dc22

                                                    2006102516

Manufactured in the United States of America

On the cover: Right: A researcher analyzes DNA samples. Left: Women in India protest the practice of sex selection.

CONTENTS

Introduction

What would you risk to know your future? Would you pay someone to tell you how you'll die? What if there were a test that would tell if you would ever have cancer? Would you take it? Would you want to know?

Imagine taking a simple blood test to learn how you'll live. But it's not that simple. The tests are rarely perfect. What they tell you may not be what you want to know. Moreover, their results can be abused. People may discriminate against you because of the secrets spelled out in your blood.

It is rare to find an advance in technology that can be used only for good. Genetic testing is no exception. In some cases, it improves lives. It helps people have healthy children. It helps

Scientists at the Reproductive Genetics Institute in Chicago use computers to diagnose genetic diseases in fetuses.

doctors provide better treatment. But genetic testing can be used in other ways as well. It can be used to take away people's jobs. It can be used to tell doctors what they cannot do instead of what they can do for an illness.

Today, lawmakers, scientists, and citizens debate how genetic testing should be regulated. When is genetic testing appropriate? When is genetic testing not appropriate? There must be a way to come to an agreement on how genetic tests should be used and how they shouldn't.

Chapter 1

Genetic Testing Defined

Human beings are made by genes. Thousands of them are translated into words of protein, sentences of cells, and paragraphs of organ systems. The language of genes tells the stories that make each of us unique. Each gene makes one protein. The way those words are spelled, cut, and combined is the reason your sister has red hair and you have blonde hair. It is why your best friend's skin is that beautiful shade of chocolate brown.

WHAT IS A GENE?

A gene is an instruction. We read a recipe in a cookbook to learn how to make rice pudding or chicken parmesan.

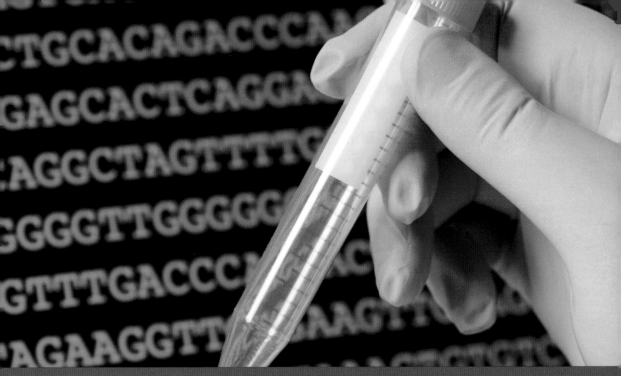

A, C, T, and G are the four letters that make up the language of DNA. In a microscopic sample, those four letters are repeated millions of times.

Proteins in our cells read our genes to make more proteins. These proteins become cells, organs, and eventually human beings. Cells speak the language of DNA. It is not a complicated language. The alphabet has only four letters—A, C, T, and G—representing the four nucleotides that make up all of DNA. All the words they spell are only three letters long. Although there are sixty-four words in the language of DNA, they have only twenty-two meanings. They say only "go," "stop," and the names of the twenty amino acids that make up all the proteins currently known to science.

Just as recipes are made of many words, so are genes. The average size of a human gene is 3,000 letters, or 1,000 words. At least one gene has been discovered that is more than two million letters long. Each gene starts with go and ends with stop. In between those simple commands is where things get interesting.

ALLELES

Chromosomes are like cookbooks. They contain the genes' instructions. Normally, humans have twenty-three pairs of chromosomes. Each one contains thousands of genes. The pairs of chromosomes are made up of one chromosome each from a person's mother and father. With one exception, each member of a pair of chromosomes contains instructions for the same proteins. These instructions are not identical. Every cook has his or her own variation of a dish. In the same way, each chromosome has its own variation of a gene. One example of this is the ability to roll your tongue from side to side. This fun skill is determined by variations of a single gene. Such differences in a gene are known as its alleles.

DOMINANT AND RECESSIVE

Sometimes a person has two alleles of a gene that are identical. These people are said to be homozygous for the trait that gene encodes. When the alleles are different, they are said to be heterozygous. What happens when a person has two different alleles? How does the body know which instruction to follow? For many traits, the answer is simple. One trait is dominant, and the other is recessive. In these cases, the dominant allele is the one that is expressed, or listened to, by the body. The recessive allele is ignored. This is the type of inheritance that leads to the 3:1 rule demonstrated in 1866 by Gregor Mendel from his studies on pea plants. Chromosomes are distributed randomly. Therefore, each child has a one in two chance of getting a copy of each allele from its parents. One trait in humans that follows this rule is dimples. Dimples (D) are dominant over not having dimples (d). Suppose both parents have dimples and the genotype Dd. Then their children could have four possible genotypes. The children could be DD, Dd, dD, or dd. The dominant allele is present in three of the four possibilities. Therefore, three times out of four, the child would have dimples. Each parent in this example would also have dimples. If one parent had no dimples, he or she would be dd. Then possible genotypes for their children would be Dd, dd, Dd, and dd. Only half their children would have dimples. This is not the only way that alleles can interact. For example, sometimes two different alleles work together. They produce an outcome that is a mixture of what each would express alone.

X-LINKED TRAITS

Why are recessive alleles overwhelmed by dominant ones? It is frequently because they contain the recipe for a protein that doesn't work. For many traits, this makes no difference. A white flower is no less beautiful than a red one. However, some proteins are essential for human health. In these cases, the 3:1 ratio is a good thing. It means that fewer children are born with problems. But the 3:1 ratio doesn't always exist. There is one set of chromosomes that doesn't always come in matched

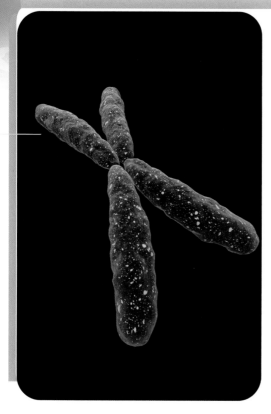

In this computer-enhanced image of a human chromosome, DNA is tightly coiled around a protein backbone, which helps the chromosome keep its shape.

pairs. These are the sex chromosomes. Women have a matched pair of two X chromosomes. Men, however, have one X and one Y. This can lead to an interesting situation. Some important genes are present on the part of the X chromosome that is not duplicated on the Y. The Y chromosome cannot balance out problems with these genes. One X chromosome with a faulty recessive gene passed on from the mother is all that it takes to cause a male child to have a problem. Traits passed on in this manner are known as X-linked traits. Scientists have known about them for many years because of how they are distributed in the population. They show up far more frequently in boys than in girls. Some examples of X-linked traits are red-green color blindness, hemophilia, and male pattern baldness.

WHAT CAUSES GENETIC DISEASE?

The process of inheritance is not perfect. Each person has his or her own unique genetic code. This code is copied in every cell of his or her body. Whenever something is copied many times, mistakes can occur. Many of these copying errors occur in the nonsense syllables that are between the genes. However, other errors occur in the words of the genes themselves. These errors are known as mutations.

MUTATIONS

There are many different types of mutations. A point mutation is a mistake where one letter is replaced with another. The code, in a point mutation, stays the same length. This is one of the safer kinds of mutations. Since all words are the same three-letter length, at most only one meaning is changed. Some amino acids can be spelled in several different ways. This means that sometimes a point mutation has no effect at all. More dangerous are those errors that change the length of the code. These are called frame shift mutations. They get their name because the entire code after the mistake will be shifted one letter to the left and therefore misread. Frame shift mutations are usually deletions or duplications of just one letter. They seem simple, but everything after them stops making sense. It's similar to what would happen if you made a typing error in the middle of a sentence and ende du pshiftin gove rth espac e.

MITOSIS, MEIOSIS, AND HOMOLOGOUS RECOMBINATION

Most cells in the body copy themselves by a process known as mitosis. During mitosis, the cell divides into two exact copies of itself. As long as the copying process doesn't make any mistakes, each copy will be identical. This is not true for the sex cells—the sperm and egg, or gametes—that will create the next generation. Gametes divide by a different process. Sperm and egg cells are made by meiosis. Instead of making two whole cells, they make four half cells. Each of these cells has a single copy of each chromosome instead of two. These chromosomes are not always the same as the chromosomes in the parent cell. This is because of a process known as homologous recombination. During homologous recombination, matched pairs of chromosomes can swap alleles. This means that the chromosomes in a person's gametes have many variations. There aren't just two.

CHROMOSOMAL ABNORMALITIES

Sometimes, the process of meiosis doesn't work properly. When this happens, it can create a sperm or egg cell with too few, or too many, chromosomes. If such gametes combine during a pregnancy, the fetus will have the wrong number of chromosomes. It may have three copies or one copy of a particular chromosome, instead of a pair. Most of the time, such a fetus cannot survive. However, because many genes are duplicated, some of these problems are less dangerous than others.

TURNER'S SYNDROME: SHOULD ALL GENETIC PROBLEMS BE THOUGHT OF AS DISEASES?

What happens when a child is born with just one X chromosome? What sex is the child? Turner's syndrome occurs when children are born with just one functioning sex chromosome—an X. A fetus with just a Y chromosome would not survive to birth. Approximately one in every 2,500 girls is born with Turner's syndrome. Children with Turner's syndrome tend to be shorter than average. Otherwise, they seem to be normal girls. Their main physical difference is that they never develop ovaries. This is clearly a genetic problem. But is it a disease? Girls with Turner's syndrome do have an increased risk of some health problems. They aren't, however, physically ill. They're just different. They live as long as other people. Most of their physical symptoms can be eliminated with hormone therapy. They can even carry children! They just need to use a donor egg. What use, for them, is genetic testing? If Turner's syndrome is diagnosed early enough, some of its physical signs can be eliminated. Girls can be given human growth hormone to grow taller. They can be treated with estrogen to help them develop breasts and other female characteristics, but it's mostly a matter of appearance.

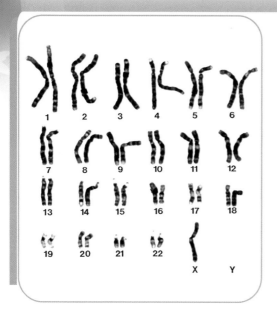

This karyotype maps out the chromosomes of a girl with Turner's syndrome. Note that she has only one X chromosome.

A PERFECT COPYING MACHINE

There have been millions of years of human evolution. Is it strange that a perfect DNA copying machine has never evolved? It actually makes perfect sense. Evolution requires humans to continue to grow and change. They couldn't do so if the machinery for copying DNA never made mistakes. It takes a mistake to move human beings to the next level. When mistakes are beneficial, their carriers survive. Then the new alleles increase in frequency in the population. When a mistake is harmful, alleles with it slowly disappear. Variation is necessary for evolution.

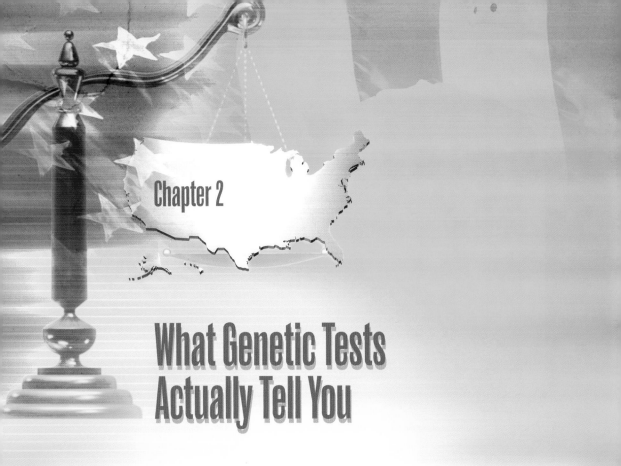

Chapter 2

What Genetic Tests Actually Tell You

A genetic test does not tell if you have a disease. It does not even tell you if you have a gene. It tells you whether you have the specific allele of a gene that is linked with a disease.

WHY WERE GENETIC TESTS DEVELOPED?

Scientists developed tests for genetic diseases when they saw that some illnesses clump in certain ethnic groups and families. One of those is the fatal disease known as Tay-Sachs disease. Infants born with it rarely live to age four. Tay-Sachs is ten times more common in Ashkenazi Jews than in the rest of the population. It is a recessive

Late nineteenth-century Ashkenazi Jews rarely married outside their community. This limited genetic diversity and increased the risk of Tay-Sachs disease.

disease. Therefore, both parents must be carriers to pass it on. But in some small communities, many people are carriers. These communities lost baby after baby until scientists learned how to test for carrier status. Tay-Sachs was one of the first genetic diseases to be tested for in large groups. The test doesn't actually require any DNA analysis. Carriers have a lower level of the protein that is affected by the disease. They can be diagnosed with a simple blood test. Suddenly, couples could be screened for carrier status. High-risk groups began to require couples to be screened before they would be allowed to marry. Now, because of genetic testing, Tay-Sachs is well on its way to being stamped out.

EARLY UNDERSTANDING OF HEREDITARY DISEASES

More than 200 years ago, scientists first realized that a disease called hemophilia ran in families. People with hemophilia can

Queen Victoria, pictured here as a young woman, is probably history's best-known carrier of a genetic disease.

lose a large amount of blood from even a small cut because of the inability of their blood to clot. It is also known as the Royal Disease. In the 1800s, it affected the interbred royal families of Europe.

Queen Victoria of England was a carrier of hemophilia. A carrier is a person who has one copy of a dangerous recessive allele. Carriers do not have the disease because they also have the dominant allele. Queen Victoria passed the dangerous allele to two of her daughters and one of her sons. Her daughters Alice and Beatrice were also carriers and married well. They passed the disease on to the German, Russian, and Spanish royal families.

Hemophilia is located on the X chromosome. This means that any male with the dangerous allele will have the disease. Males cannot be carriers because they have no second X chromosome to mask the trait. The queen's son Leopold was the first royal hemophiliac.

A PROBLEM FOR MODERN FAMILIES

More recently, another genetic disease became famous. It helped scientists understand how DNA is copied. Huntington's disease slowly destroys the brain. Over time, people with the disease lose the ability to speak, walk, and even think. Huntington's is unlike most other genetic diseases. The mutation for it is dominant. Everyone with the Huntington's allele eventually gets sick. Although it may seem surprising, this doesn't prevent the disease from being passed. Most people don't get sick until they are in their 30s or 40s. By this time, many have already had children.

The mutation that causes Huntington's disease is the result of a specific copying error. This type of error is known as expansion of a triplet repeat. Sometimes, in your DNA, there is a word that is repeated several times. This signals for the use of the same amino acid multiple times in a row. When reading this type of DNA, sometimes the copying machinery slips and makes more copies of the word than it should. The more copies of the CAG code that a person has, the more likely the copy machine will make a mistake. Also, the more copies of the CAG code a person has, the earlier he or she starts to get sick. Healthy people have six to thirty copies of the CAG code. Those with Huntington's disease may have eighty or more copies.

WHAT DOES A POSITIVE TEST MEAN?

A doctor says that you have tested positive for a genetic disease. What does that mean? It depends on the disease. It also depends

Dr. Nancy Wexler examines a genetic chart of families with Huntington's disease. Her research helped scientists identify the location of the faulty Huntington gene.

on the test. Why is a positive test so hard to interpret? There are many reasons. The test may not be perfect. Just having the gene might not mean that you are definitely going to get sick.

PENETRANCE

Penetrance is how scientists figure out what it means to have a dangerous gene. It asks how likely it is that the mutation will affect your health. Huntington's disease has 100 percent penetrance. Everyone who has the gene will get the disease. Most diseases are not as easy to explain. Some diseases have many genes linked with them. In this case, even a dominant mutation might not always cause the disease. Other genes

SENSITIVITY, SPECIFICITY, AND PREDICTIVE VALUE

Scientists have developed tests called sensitivity, specificity, and predictive value in order to understand what tests mean. Sensitivity is a way to judge how well a test identifies sick people. If a test has 90 percent sensitivity, nine out of ten sick people will test positive. Specificity is the opposite test. It looks at how well a test identifies healthy people. If a test has 80 percent specificity, then eight out of ten healthy people will test negative. These numbers are very useful for the people who create the tests. They're not very useful for the person taking them. Why not? The doctor has no way of telling what a patient's positive test means. Is he one of the nine sick people with a correct result? Or is he one of the two healthy people with an incorrect one? What they need to know is the predictive value of the test. The predictive value takes into account the sensitivity and specificity of the test. It also looks at how common the disease is. This allows it to answer the most useful question of all. If a patient tests positive, what is the chance he or she is actually sick?

A doctor explains the meaning of a test result to one of his patients. Even effective genetic screening tests can have errors or inconclusive results.

might stop the mutation from being turned on. They could also make proteins to cancel out its effects. Genes with 100 percent penetrance are rare. Inheritance of most genetic disorders is far from simple.

POSITIVE DOES NOT ALWAYS MEAN SICK

Sometimes, a positive test means you will get sick. Most of the time, a positive test isn't so black and white. It may just mean you are at greater risk of disease than other people. A positive test for one of the "breast cancer genes" does not mean you will get breast cancer. Between 35 and 85 percent of women with BRCA1 or BRCA2 get breast cancer. In contrast, 14 percent of women who don't have one of these breast cancer genes get breast cancer. However, less than 10 percent of all breast cancers occur in women with one of the breast cancer genes. This is because most women do not have the gene. Women without the gene have lower risk, but there are many more of them who can become sick. Test results are not simple. Sometimes, a negative test doesn't mean that you are certain to stay healthy.

It is hard to make a smart decision about whether to undergo a genetic test. To do so, people must be aware of what these tests mean. They must understand the difference between risk and certainty. They need to know that results are rarely a guarantee. They need to research what options they have for dealing with the results. Just like with other tests, it always pays to do your homework before taking them.

Chapter 3

Building a Better Baby: The Positive Side of Prenatal Testing

Many young couples dream of starting a family. They imagine they will have perfect children. They hope for children who are healthy. They long for children who will fulfill their dreams. For some couples, the process is different. They are as afraid as they are hopeful. They worry about who their children will be. Perhaps they have already had a child with a serious genetic illness. Maybe one of their nieces or nephews died at a young age. Or they could be from a group with a high risk of inheritable disease. For these couples, genetic testing can ease the heart and mind. Simple blood tests

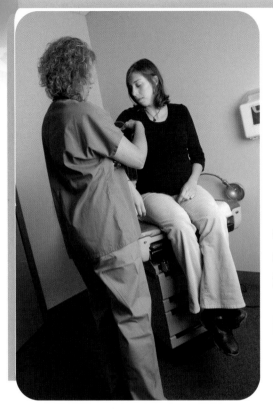

Doctors can perform multiple prenatal screening tests on a blood sample provided by the mother.

can determine whether they are likely to pass on serious illnesses to their children.

PRENATAL TESTING FOR INHERITABLE DISORDERS

There are two ways to test for inheritable diseases. The parents can be tested or the fetus can be tested. The advantage of testing the parents is that the test poses little or no risk. They can discover if either of them carries the genes they are worried about. Then they can choose whether or not to risk having a child. The problem with testing the parents is that it rarely gives a definite answer. It just lets them know how likely they are to have a child with the disease.

Dominant mutations cause the disease in any person who has them. Sometimes, diseases caused by dominant mutations make people sick before they are old enough to have children. In that case, they know their children will be at risk. Any child would have at least a one in two chance of having the disease. Why would you need to test for this kind of disease? Because the best-known disease caused by a dominant mutation makes people sick after their childbearing years. People may want to be tested for the Huntington's gene because they've seen how the disease affects their mother or father. They may want to know for the sake of their own future.

Sometimes prenatal testing is not just for the sake of the children. For a dominant mutation, it is easy to calculate the probabilities. If either parent has a single copy of the gene, then any child they have has a one in two chance of inheriting it. If either parent has two copies of the mutation, then any child will definitely inherit it. If both parents have a single copy of the mutation, the probability that their child will have the illness is three out of four.

With a recessive mutation, a person must inherit two copies of the gene in order to get sick. If only one parent has only one copy of the gene, there is no chance that their children will get sick. Half of their children, however, will be carriers of the mutation. If both parents have a single copy of the gene, the probabilities are different. Half the children will be carriers. A quarter of their children will be healthy. Another quarter will have the disease. A one in four chance of a fatal illness is a scary prospect. Many couples in this situation choose to adopt a child. They may also use donated sperm or eggs from someone who does not carry the trait.

There is only way to be certain whether a child will have a genetic disease: The developing embryo must be tested. There are two ways to do this. The first is called amniocentesis.

Amniocentesis removes some of the fluid from around the growing baby. It can be done between fifteen and twenty weeks of pregnancy. The second testing method is known as chorionic villus sampling. It samples some of the tissue from the placenta. It can be done between ten and twelve weeks of pregnancy.

PRENATAL TESTING FOR CHROMOSOMAL DISORDERS

Some genetic disorders can only be tested for after a child has been conceived. For example, parents cannot be tested for disorders of meiosis. These occur when there is a mistake with cell division. In these cases, there are no mutated genes. Instead, the sperm or egg cell has the wrong number of chromosomes. A child may end up with a piece of an extra chromosome, or a whole extra chromosome. A child might also end up missing all or part of a chromosome. Chromosome disorders are detected by a test called a karyotype. Doctors remove one of the baby's cells and take a light micrograph picture of the chromosomes. Then the chromosomes are counted. Most chromosomal disorders are either fatal or cause serious health problems. Therefore, many parents want to test for them as early as possible. At that point, they can make an informed decision about whether to continue the pregnancy.

TOO MANY OR TOO FEW

It is almost always fatal to be missing a chromosome. Having an extra chromosome is also a problem. This condition is called

Aya Iwamoto has Down syndrome, a genetic disorder caused by trisomy 21. She also has a college degree.

a trisomy. *Trisomy* is derived from the prefix for three ("tri") and the root, "somy," which is Greek for "relating to the body." A child with a trisomy has three copies of a chromosome instead of a pair. Trisomies include Down syndrome (chromosome 21), Patau's syndrome (chromosome 13), and Edward's syndrome (chromosome 18.) Most babies with trisomy conditions die within a few months of birth, if not sooner. Down syndrome is an exception.

Extra or missing sex chromosomes are rarely fatal. All a child needs is one X chromosome to live a life of normal length. There is only one way that a person can be missing a whole chromosome and survive. This is monosomy X ("mono" means one). Children with Turner's syndrome *(see p. 13)* have a single X chromosome.

BITS AND PIECES

There are other types of chromosomal disorders. Not just whole chromosomes can be misplaced. So can bits and pieces. This happens when chromosomes are broken. There are three types of chromosomal damage. An extra piece of chromosome is called an addition. This is the cause of the most common form of mental retardation. Fragile X is due to an extra piece attached to the end of one X chromosome. Deletion, a second type of chromosome damage, occurs when there is a missing piece of chromosome. Most deletions are fatal. Cri du chat is one deletion that isn't. Children with cri du chat are missing a small piece of chromosome 5. They have severe mental retardation and small heads. Their cries sound like those of a cat, which is how the disorder got its name (*cri du chat* means "cat's cry" in French). Finally, there are translocations. This is when one chromosome ends up with a piece of a different one stuck to it by mistake. Everything is still there; it's just in the wrong place. This can cause problems because a gene's location can affect how it works. The most common type of leukemia, a blood cancer, seen in the United States is due to a translocation.

PREIMPLANTATION TESTING

Science has given some parents a better option. Their own sperm and eggs can be used to make embryos outside of their bodies. This is known as in vitro fertilization (IVF). Embryos made by IVF can be easily tested for genetic diseases. After testing, only the healthy ones are put in the mother's uterus.

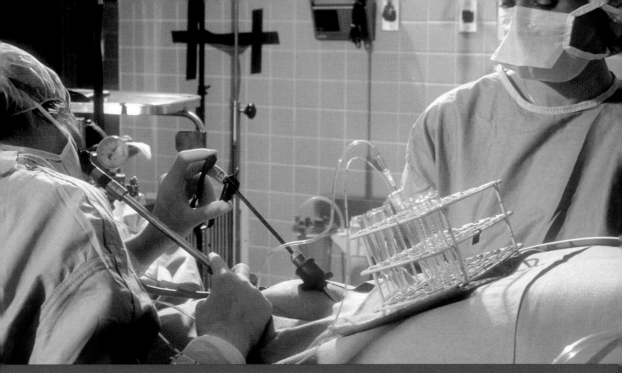

Doctors remove ova (eggs) from a woman who is planning to have a baby through in vitro fertilization.

There is then no need to do genetic tests during pregnancy. IVF reduces the risk of pregnancy loss. Sometimes, parents are worried about genetic diseases but are against abortion. For them, preimplantation testing may be an acceptable choice. Some doctors suggest this type of testing for everyone undergoing IVF. Preimplantation testing raises the chance of having a healthy baby.

SHOULD ALL DISEASES BE TESTED FOR?

Before testing a pregnancy for the presence of a genetic disorder, parents need to think about what they will do if the test result is positive. In most cases, the options are black and white. They will either continue the pregnancy or abort. What people choose to do depends on several issues. Would the disease be fatal? Does a positive test mean there is a 100 percent chance the child will be ill? How would the illness change the child's quality of life? The answers aren't always simple. For example, many children with Down syndrome are able to live long and

THE ABORTION DEBATE AND THE GENETIC TESTING DEBATE

Why do people test a fetus for genetic illnesses? Some do so to be prepared for any problems. Others do so because they don't want a sick child. This is why genetic testing is linked with the abortion debate. Some people want to be able to end a problem pregnancy. That, to them, is the point of testing. This is why some pro-life people are against genetic testing. There is often nothing you can do to treat a genetic disease before birth. Therefore, if you are against abortion, there is no reason to test. Several pro-life groups have proposed laws on genetic testing. They would forbid any genetic test that could lead to an abortion. Prenatal testing also worries disability advocates. It doesn't matter if they are pro-choice. They believe that disability should not affect a child's right to be born. Many people question if there is a line. Does it matter what you are testing for? Is it really wrong to test for a disease that would kill a child within a few months of birth? How is that different from testing for one that would affect only the child's quality of life?

fulfilled lives, with a minimum of problems. Others are not. So, what should a parent do? It is up to each individual. For some people, it is better not to have the testing done at all. If they are unwilling to intervene in the case of a problem, there is little point to finding out about it a few months early. This is particularly true because of the problems with false positive and false negative tests. As we learned earlier, few scientific tests are perfect. There is generally a small but significant chance that a test has given the wrong result.

What about testing after birth? Newborns can be screened for many treatable genetic disorders, some of which can cause major health problems if not caught right away. These include disorders of how they digest food. Most states require doctors to test for some, or all, of these conditions. Today, children are much less likely to have life-long damage from problems that could have been avoided. This has been one of the triumphs of genetic testing.

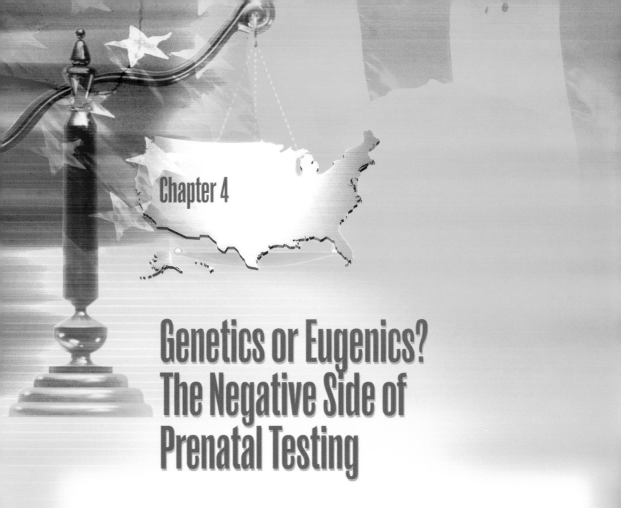

Chapter 4

Genetics or Eugenics?
The Negative Side of
Prenatal Testing

P renatal genetic testing could do at least as much
harm as it does good. Parents are unlikely to select
for diversity in their children. They want children who
are smart, healthy, and more beautiful. Over time, these
"positive" traits could be increased in the population.
Specific genes linked with good outcomes would be selected
over others. What if society changes? It is harder for a
uniform population to adapt. That is the irony in trying
to create a race of perfect children. Without diversity,
there is no evolution.

In 2006, Stephen Hawking *(center)* received the Royal Society Copley Medal for scientific achievement. He overcame his disability to become a celebrated astrophysicist.

WHO ARE WE TO DETERMINE WHAT LIFE IS WORTH LIVING?

All technology leads to ethical questions. Prenatal genetic testing is no exception. It may even lead to more questions than most. For example: Who has the right to determine who should be born? This question is particularly important to the disabled, especially when scientists make controversial statements, such as, "We could prevent any more deaf children from being born." This sends the message to deaf people that the world sees them as defective. They are viewed as having less value. People with disabilities can contribute just as

IN VITRO FERTILIZATION AND MALE CYSTIC FIBROSIS CARRIERS

Cystic fibrosis (CF) is a genetic disease. It causes the lungs to become sticky and clogged with mucus. Half of all individuals with CF die before they turn forty. It is a very serious disease. Until recently, few people with CF lived to adulthood.

CF is caused by a recessive mutation. It takes two copies of the mutant gene to cause the disease. Men who are carriers have only one copy of the gene. They don't show obvious signs of the disease. They are, however, frequently infertile. It takes a doctor's help for them to become fathers. To do this, their sperm is removed using a needle. Then the doctor can use it to fertilize an egg.

Sometimes men do not know that they are infertile because they are carriers of CF. This can cause problems. Technology has enabled them to pass on the dangerous mutation. Because of this, the CF gene is becoming more common. Until recently, a carrier's infertility made it a difficult gene to pass on. Today, most doctors have learned to tell infertile men to get tested for the gene. That way, they can determine if they could be passing it on to their children. Some men still choose to father children using in vitro fertilization. In that case, their partners should be tested for carrier status. The embryo can be tested as well.

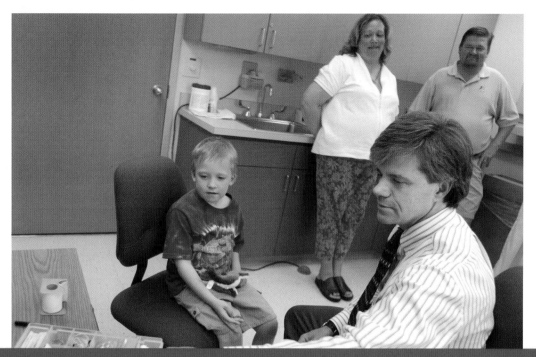

A young boy with cystic fibrosis receives treatment for his condition. CF is the most common genetic disease among people of European descent.

much as anyone else. Sometimes their unique insights can help them do even more.

Some people say that it is kind to abort fetuses that might be born disabled. They say that it is cruel to make a child live with such problems. Most people with disabilities would disagree. They're glad that they were born. Are there any genetic diseases where it really is worse to be born? Some genetic disorders kill most or all of their victims within a few months. That is a hard life for both parents and child. However, treatment is always improving. In the 1960s, the average lifespan for children with cystic fibrosis (CF) was only ten years. In 2005, half of all people with CF lived past thirty-five. These decisions are not black and white. Not even in the most extreme cases. In some

The Nazis believed they could breed a pure "master race" through eugenics. They viewed healthy, young Germans as the best examples of humanity.

cases, not allowing a child to be born probably is the best decision. The problem is, how do you know?

THE HISTORICAL HORRORS

The term "eugenics" was coined in the late 1800s for the study of improving the human race by controlling breeding. In the early 1900s, the eugenic movement became extremely popular. Laws were passed across most of the United States, encouraging the forced sterilization of people with disabilities. Scientists who practiced eugenics thought they were doing good things. They wanted to improve humanity. However, eugenics led to many horrors. Some of Adolf Hitler's most horrible acts were done in the name of eugenics. Moreover, the horrors are not so far in the past. It was only in 1967 that the U.S. Supreme Court struck down the laws forbidding people of different races to marry.

Many critics of genetic testing think it could make eugenics easier. What if there were a way to test for "better" traits? What would stop people from selecting for them? It is clearly wrong to stop someone from having children just because he or she is short. It seems normal to choose a spouse who is smart and beautiful. How do we define the line? Is it when parents decide to implant only those embryos that have the gene for red hair? Is it when they abort any fetus that would be born a girl?

THE CURRENT DILEMMAS

The last question is not an idle one. Sex selection by abortion is common in many Asian countries. Sex selection has been illegal in China since 1995. However, in 2000, there were more than 130 boys born for each 100 girls in some areas of the country. The normal ratio is 102/100. Sex selection is not the only questionable use of genetic testing today. Some parents who have seriously ill children use genetic testing to try and save their lives by conceiving a second child. They select for an embryo with the same blood type. But they choose one without the gene that causes the illness. They try to create a child who can serve as an organ donor. For some couples, it is their best chance to save their first child's life. Sometimes, doctors will help in this process. They screen many embryos to find the one that will be the closest match. What happens, though, when the new child is born? What if she doesn't want to have surgery to help her older sister? Is it ethical for her parents to force her to donate bone marrow? What about a kidney or a piece of her liver? Is it fair for parents to conceive one child

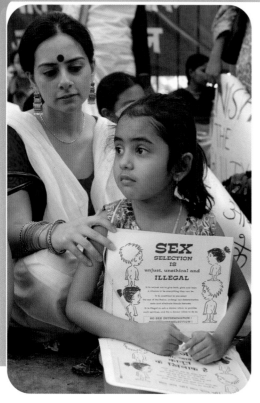

At a rally in New Delhi, India, activists protest the illegal but widespread practice of sex selection.

just to help save another? They may love their new child just as much, but how would it feel to learn that that was why you were born?

THE FUTURE

Genetic technology is constantly improving. Soon amazing feats may be possible. We could create children with amazing stamina. Children who are all beautiful. Children who learn incredibly fast. Over time, scientists are learning more and more about which genes control which traits. One day soon, it may be easy to select for children with the traits a parent wants. Even if this sort of genetic selection doesn't have unintended consequences for the child herself, it could for society.

There are many concerns about using genetic testing to try and create perfect children. One worry is that it could create a genetic elite. Children of wealth have economic advantages, allowing them better access to health and opportunities. In the future, wealthy children could have genetic advantages as well. Over time, access to genetic technology could create a new kind of aristocracy. These children would be smarter and healthier, and would live longer than their counterparts. This could cement the status differences already found in society. In this type of future, it would be harder for people born to poor parents to pull themselves up by their bootstraps. Currently, people all basically have the same internal resources to draw on. But what happens in a society where some are born stronger or faster? What happens if some are more intelligent? How will those not given these advantages compete?

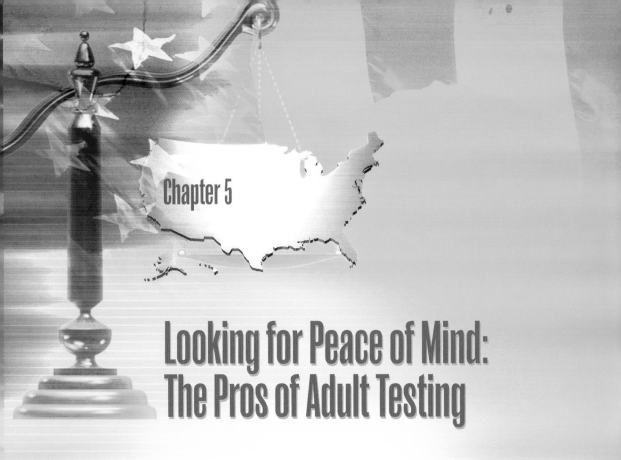

Chapter 5

Looking for Peace of Mind: The Pros of Adult Testing

G enetic testing allows adults to plan for their lives. It can be helpful for people to know they are at high risk of disease. It may change the way they seek care. Early diagnosis can mean the difference between life and death. For example, women make different choices when they are at high risk for breast cancer. They start getting mammograms at a younger age. Normally, women do not get mammograms until they are forty. Women with the breast cancer genes are advised to start getting them earlier. This type of test for breast cancer uses X-rays and may slightly increase the risk of disease. But for high-risk women, the danger is balanced out. The possibility of early diagnosis is worth the risk of

Doctors at the Comprehensive Cancer Center at the University of California, San Francisco, review mammograms (breast X-rays) for signs of cancer.

more frequent testing. The earlier cancer is treated, the more likely it can be cured.

TESTING FOR ADULT-ONSET DISEASES

In adults, genetic testing is usually done for one of three reasons. It can be done to diagnose a genetic disease. It can be done to assess the risk of getting a genetic disease. Finally, it can be done to see if people are carriers of a genetic disease. Carriers will not get sick, but they might pass the disease on to their children.

When most people think of genetic testing, they think of predictive testing. This is testing that determines a person's risk of becoming ill. However, a positive test result does not always mean you will get sick.

CURABLE AND TREATABLE DISEASES

Two types of genetic diseases can be tested for in adults: curable and incurable diseases. People test for them for different reasons. For treatable diseases, there are advantages to knowing you are at high risk. You can change your life to reduce your risk factors. Your doctor can start screening you at a younger age. She can also screen you more often to make it less likely that symptoms will be missed. This type of genetic testing may not be appropriate for children and adolescents. It depends on when the disease usually sets in. For several reasons, doctors recommend against genetic testing for most late-onset diseases until adulthood. It can be hard for a child to understand what the test means. Also, most of the time, nothing useful can be done until adulthood.

There is another reason for people to seek out predictive testing. Sometimes, they can be treated to reduce the chance they will get sick. This is called prophylactic treatment. Prophylactic treatment can be drug treatment. It can also be surgery to remove the tissue where the disease is most likely to strike.

INCURABLE DISEASES

Would you want to know you were going to get a horrible illness if you could not treat it or avoid it? Some people say no. Others say yes. They want to have time to prepare. They may want to

THE CONTROVERSY OVER PROPHYLACTIC MASTECTOMY

"An ounce of prevention is worth a pound of cure" is an old folk saying that is frequently true. It is usually easier to prevent diseases than to cure them. What about a pound of prevention? Can you ever do too much to avoid disease? Some people think so. Recently, some women at high genetic risk for breast cancer have decided to undergo a new procedure known as prophylactic mastectomy. In this surgery, doctors remove the breasts before any disease has occurred. On one hand, this makes sense. Breast tissue that isn't there cannot become cancerous. After surgery, the chance of cancer is reduced by over 90 percent. On the other hand, this is major surgery. There is the possibility of severe complications. Removal of the breasts can cause both mental and physical problems. There is also a chance that these people never would have developed cancer. Doctors rarely recommend this procedure. It is generally suggested in only two types of cases: extremely high risk of disease or if there could be problems with treatment or detection. Some women choose this surgery for another reason. They are terrified by the possibility that they might get cancer. Removal of their breasts seems like a small price to pay for peace of mind.

Some people want to know their risks of genetic disease so that they can plan for any changes they may have to make as they get older.

know if their work life will be affected by the disease or if they have a limited time before they become disabled. They may want to know if it is safe for them to have children. They may want the test so that they can stop worrying. Sometimes, knowing you will get sick is less stressful than worrying. In general, adults have the right to decide whether they want or need such information. What about children? Most doctors say that children should wait until they are capable of making their own informed choice. Testing should not be their parents' decision. For a child, learning the result of a test can affect self-esteem. It can also affect relationships with parents and siblings. Often there is no advantage to testing other than to relieve parents' worries. Therefore, there is no reason not to wait.

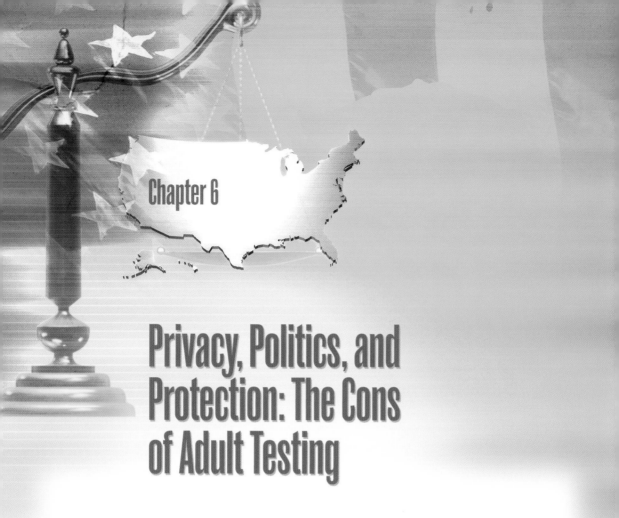

Chapter 6

Privacy, Politics, and Protection: The Cons of Adult Testing

The right to privacy is guaranteed by the constitution. There is nothing more personal than your genetic code. Do you have the right to keep it private? Many companies have decided that you don't. All types of institutions have performed genetic testing on people without their consent.

WORKPLACE DISCRIMINATION

The United States has a long history of genetic discrimination. Early immigration policies were designed to

A scientist studies the results of a DNA test. Who has the right to know the results of these tests?

bring only the strongest stock into the country. The forced sterilization and anti–racial-mixing laws of the early twentieth century were designed to improve future generations. Now there are issues of genetic discrimination in the workplace. Employers may not want to hire someone who is at risk of health problems. Those future health problems could cost an employer money. Employers do not worry only about health care. They could lose money when someone sick misses work. Early retirement is expensive, too. It takes time and money to train someone's replacement. It is to the employers' benefit to hire the healthiest people. Several companies have gotten into trouble for running genetic screening tests on employees without their consent. However, in many states, this is actually legal.

Health insurance costs are a large portion of company expenses. Each year, costs go up. Companies must do whatever they can in order to afford coverage. Eliminating high-risk employees makes their costs go down. Genetic testing can seem like just another way to save money.

INSURANCE DISCRIMINATION

Imagine if just knowing that you were at risk for a disease meant you could never get treatment. Insurance companies are in the business of minimizing risk. Often, they do not cover preexisting conditions, which are health problems that a person had before trying to get insurance.

PRIVATE INSURANCE

Insurance companies bet that they will take in more money than they will pay out. Therefore, they are picky about whom they'll enroll. Most adults in the United States have insurance through their work. Covering a company's employees is a good bet for the insurer. People who work regular jobs are generally healthy. It also spreads out the risk. There are a lot of healthy people paying in the company. Probably very few will get seriously ill. It's harder for people who need to buy their own insurance. Any risk factors cause them to be charged more. Some cause them to be denied coverage altogether.

Can genetic testing cause people to be denied insurance? It has already happened. Sometimes, a person with a positive genetic test does get new coverage. Then the person just has

I'VE BEEN WORKING ON THE RAILROAD

Being a railroad engineer is hard work. Railroad engineers have lots of injuries. One common injury is known as carpal tunnel syndrome. This is a type of damage to the nerves of the wrist. It happens when jobs require a lot of repeated hand movements. In one year, more than 100 workers at a railroad company reported having carpal tunnel syndrome. They had gotten it from doing their jobs. There are rules about what to do when someone gets hurt at work. Companies must report it to the government. Then they must pay workers' compensation. The railroad company managers did not report the injuries because they did not want to pay the money. They then had to prove that the carpal tunnel syndrome was not work-related. They tried to show it was genetic. They tested the workers for a genetic disease that had similar symptoms. It wasn't a lot like carpal tunnel syndrome, but they hoped to use it to explain the injuries. However, no one had the disease. They kept searching, but the tests were done without the workers' permission. When the workers' union found out what the company was doing, a lawsuit was filed. Eventually, the case was settled out of court. The company agreed to stop the testing and destroy all the records. It also promised to help lobby the federal government to prevent other companies from doing the same thing.

to worry if the insurance company will refuse to pay for care linked with the gene. If the insurer refuses, it is genetic discrimination. A positive genetic test isn't a preexisting condition. If anything, it is a possible future condition. However, insurance companies like to save money. The government passed the Health Insurance Portability and Accountability Act (HIPAA) in 1996, making it illegal to treat genetic mutations as preexisting conditions. Yet, many companies still find ways not to have to pay for related diseases. People are actually harmed by being smart about their health. Imagine a person with the gene that causes thickening of the heart muscle. What if the person was not screened for the gene? Then the insurer would fully cover the eventual heart attack. But what about someone who had been screened? He might have changed his diet. He might have started exercising. He might have improved his cardiac health. He might be denied coverage for his treatment just because he had been tested. Many states have passed laws prohibiting some types of genetic discrimination. Unfortunately, there are still loopholes that need to be closed.

IT RUNS IN THE FAMILY

A genetic test does not affect only you. Your family is also tested with you. It is one thing to know your mother has breast cancer. It is another to learn she has one of the breast cancer genes. One is a reflection of only her risk. The other looks at the risk of the whole family. What should you do if you learn that you are a carrier of a genetic disease? Should you tell your family? If you have an at-risk gene, it most likely came from

All expecting couples hope they will have a healthy baby. In the future, genetic testing will probably be used to make sure more babies are born healthy.

one of your parents. Each of your siblings has a 50 percent chance of having it as well. It can be hard to tell your sisters you tested positive for a disease gene. Sometimes, they do not want to know. Imagine if one of your cousins were diagnosed with Huntington's disease. You would like to be tested for the gene. You want to know if you are at risk. You discuss it with your brother. He says, "I don't want to know. I don't think you should get tested. What if you find out you're positive? Then I'll be worried, too." What would you say to him? Even if you're positive for the gene, it does not mean he will be. However, it does mean that one of your parents will get sick. Would you tell them? What if they did not want to know? Then you could not even share your result. Would it be worth getting the test if your family could not support you? These are issues that people must consider before they get a genetic test. The results don't just affect one life. They affect the lives of whole families.

SELF LIMITING

Would you change your life if you knew your genetic inheritance? What if you knew that one day you would have difficulty moving around? Would you choose a job that required physical dexterity? What if you had evidence that your children would all get a devastating brain disease? Would you choose, instead, to adopt? Genetic testing isn't a window on the future. Before people use genetic tests to make life-changing decisions, they need to understand how little the tests actually tell them.

Timeline

1819	Queen Victoria is born and is a carrier for hemophilia. Her children will pass the mutation on to many of the royal families of Europe.
1859	Darwin publishes *The Origin of Species*.
1866	Mendel demonstrates how traits are inherited using pea plants.
1872	A paper is published describing the heredity patterns of Huntington's disease.
1907	First sterilization law passed in the United States to stop people "unfit to breed" from having children.
1927	U.S. Supreme Court upholds the right of the states to pass laws mandating sterilization.
1953	Watson and Crick discover the structure of DNA.
1958	The protein mutation that causes sickle-cell disease is discovered.
1970	Maryland begins screening for carriers of Tay-Sachs disease.
1975	North Carolina passes a law prohibiting discrimination against the carriers of sickle-cell disease and hemoglobin C (another recessive blood disorder).
1978	First successful test-tube baby is born.
1983	The first genetic test for a disease is developed. It tests for Huntington's.

1986   The first automatic DNA sequencer is brought to market.

1989   The gene responsible for cystic fibrosis is discovered.

1990   The first gene therapy trial is started in the United States.

1994   Discovery of BRCA1, the "breast cancer gene."

2000   Scientists from the Human Genome Project announce they have completed a "draft" of the sequence of the human genome.

2001   Two groups of scientists independently announce that humans have approximately 30,000 genes.

2006   Scientists announce the success of a preliminary gene therapy trial for Parkinson's disease.

Glossary

allele One of several variants of a gene.

bases The nucleotides that make up DNA: adenine, thymine, guanine, and cytosine.

carrier A person who has a copy of the gene associated with a disease but who does not have the disease.

cell The basic structural unit of life.

chromosome A strand of DNA that carries numerous genes. Humans have forty-six chromosomes: twenty-two pairs of homologous, or matching, chromosomes and one pair of sex chromosomes.

DNA Deoxyribonucleic acid. The material that carries the instructions for life. Made out of bases.

dominant allele An allele that, when present in the genome, will determine the trait it describes.

embryo Initial developmental stage of a fertilized egg.

eugenics The science of improving the human race through controlled breeding.

fetus Later developmental stage of a fertilized egg.

genotype The specific gene variants that a person carries.

hereditary Passed biologically from parent to child.

heterozygous Describing two different alleles of the gene for a particular trait.

homologous recombination The swapping of DNA between sister chromosomes; the process of replacing a piece of DNA with another piece that has a similar sequence.

homozygous Describing two of the same alleles of a gene for a particular trait.

meiosis The type of cell division that results in four daughter cells, each one with half the DNA of the parent cell.

mitosis The type of cell division that results in two identical copies of the parent cell.

monosomy The condition of having a single chromosome instead of a pair. The only survivable monosomy is monosomy X. This is also known as Turner's syndrome.

organ A structure with a distinct function that is made up of several kinds of tissue. For example, the heart is an organ.

penetrance Likelihood that a gene will produce a specific effect.

preexisting condition A disease someone was diagnosed with before he or she got health insurance.

prenatal The period of time leading up to, and during, a woman's pregnancy. Prenatal means "before birth."

protein A compound whose structure is described by DNA; a linear combination of amino acids.

recessive allele An allele whose trait is expressed only if the person has two copies of the allele. The effect associated with a recessive allele is not expressed if the dominant allele of the same gene is present.

sex chromosome The X and Y chromosomes. The presence or absence of a Y chromosome determines a person's genetic sex.

tissue A structure made up of a group of similar cells that have a specific function. For example, fat is tissue.

trisomy The condition of having three chromosomes instead of a pair. Down syndrome is also known as trisomy 21.

For More Information

The ALS Association
27001 Agoura Road, Suite 150
Calabasas Hills, CA 91301-5104
(818) 880-9007
Web site: http://www.alsa.org

The American Board of Genetic Counselors
ABGC Administrative Office
9650 Rockville Pike
Bethesda, MD 20814-3998
(301) 634-7315
E-mail: info@abgc.net
Web site: http://www.abgc.net

The American Cancer Society
P.O. Box 22718
Oklahoma City, OK 73123-1718
(800) ACS-2345 (227-2345)
Web site: http://www.cancer.org

The American Civil Liberties Union
125 Broad Street, 18th Floor
New York, NY 10004
(888) 567-ACLU (2258)
Web site: http://www.aclu.org

Cystic Fibrosis Foundation
6931 Arlington Road
Bethesda, MD 20814
(800) FIGHT-CF (344-4823)
E-mail: info@cff.org
Web site: http://www.cff.org

Huntington's Disease Society of America
505 Eighth Avenue, Suite 902
New York, NY 10018
(800) 345-HDSA (4372)
E-mail: hdsainfo@hdsa.org
Web site: http://www.hdsa.org

National Down Syndrome Society
666 Broadway
New York, NY 10012
(800) 221-4602
E-mail: info@ndss.org
Web site: http://www.ndss.org

National Society of Genetic Counselors
401 N. Michigan Avenue
Chicago, IL 60611
(312) 321-6834
E-mail: nsgc@nsgc.org
Web site: http://www.nsgc.org

National Tay-Sachs & Allied Diseases Association
2001 Beacon Street, Suite 204
Boston, MA 02135
(800) 906-8723
Web site: http://www.ntsad.org

The Turner Syndrome Society of the United States
14450 T. C. Jester, Suite 260
Houston, TX 77014
(800) 365-9944
Web site: http://www.turner-syndrome-us.org

WEB SITES

Due to the changing nature of Internet links, Rosen Publishing has developed an online list of Web sites related to the subject of this book. This site is updated regularly. Please use this link to access the list:

http://www.rosenlinks.com/ad/adgt

For Further Reading

Brynie, Faith Hickman. *101 Questions About Reproduction: Or How 1 + 1 = 3 or 4 or More*. Minneapolis, MN: Twenty-First Century Books, 2006.

Cefrey, Holly. *Cloning and Genetic Engineering*. New York, NY: Rosen Book Works, 2002.

Edelson, Edward. *Gregor Mendel: And the Roots of Genetics* (Oxford Portraits in Science). New York, NY: Oxford University Press, 1999.

Freedman, Jeri. *How Do We Know About Genetics and Heredity*. New York, NY: The Rosen Publishing Group, 2005.

Fridell, Ron. *Decoding Life: Unraveling the Mysteries of the Genome*. Minneapolis, MN: Lerner Publications Company, 2005.

Johnson, Rebecca L. *Genetics*. Minneapolis, MN: Twenty-First Century Books, 2006.

Knowles, Johanna. *Huntington's Disease*. New York, NY: The Rosen Publishing Group, 2007.

Lee, Justin. *Everything You Need to Know About Cystic Fibrosis*. New York, NY: The Rosen Publishing Group, 2001.

Murphy, Wendy. *Orphan Diseases*. Brookfield, CT: Twenty-First Century Books, 2002.

Walker, Julie. *Tay-Sachs Disease*. New York, NY: The Rosen Publishing Group, 2007.

Bibliography

American Society of Human Genetics Board of Directors. "Points to Consider: Ethical Legal and Psychosocial Implications of Genetic Testing in Children and Adolescents." *American Journal of Human Genetics*, Vol. 57, 1995, pp. 1233–1241.

Andrews, Lori B., Jane E. Fullarton, Neil A. Holtzman, and Arno G. Motulsky, eds. *Assessing Genetic Risks: Implications for Health and Social Policy.* Washington, DC: National Academy Press, 1994.

Aronova-Tiuntseva, Yelena, and Clyde Freeman Herreid. *Hemophilia: "The Royal Disease."* National Center for Case Study Teaching in Science, State University of New York University at Buffalo. Retrieved December 13, 2006 (http://www.sciencecases.org/hemo/hemo.asp).

Burke, Wylie. "Genetic Testing." *New England Journal of Medicine*, Vol. 347, No. 23, December 2002, pp. 1867–1875.

Collins, Francis S. *A Brief Primer on Genetic Testing.* World Economic Forum. January 24, 2004. Retrieved December 13, 2006 (http://www.genome.gov/page.cfm?pageID=10506784).

Danzinger, Kari L., Lauri D. Black, Steven B. Keiles, Anja Kammesheidt, and Paul J. Turek. "Improved Detection of Cystic Fibrosis Mutations in Infertility Patients with DNA Sequence Analysis." *Human Reproduction*, Vol. 19, No. 3, March 2004, pp. 540–546.

Gridley, Deborah. "Genetic Testing Under the ADA: A Case for Protection from Employment Discrimination." *Georgetown*

Law Journal, April 2001. Retrieved December 13, 2006 (http://www.findarticles.com/p/articles/mi_qa3805/is_200104/ai_n8936821).

Khamsi, Roxanne. "Gene Profiling Boosts Tailored Chemotherapy." NewScientist.com. October, 22, 2006. Retrieved December 13, 2006 (http://www.newscientist.com/article/dn10346-gene-profiling-boosts-tailored-chemotherapy.html).

Lorenz, Eva. "Predictive Testing in the Workplace—Could the German Model Serve as a Blueprint for Uniform Legislation in the United States?" *North Carolina Journal of Law and Technology*, Vol. 7, No. 2, Spring 2006, pp. 487–527.

MacMillan, Leigh. "Tailored Drugs on the Horizon: VUMC Study." *The Reporter*. March 28, 2003. Retrieved December 13, 2006 (http://www.mc.vanderbilt.edu/reporter/index.html?ID=2587).

National Cancer Institute. "Genetic Testing for BRCA1 and BRCA2: It's Your Choice." National Cancer Institute Fact Sheet. 2003. Retrieved December 13, 2006 (http://www.cancer.gov/cancertopics/factsheet/Risk/BRCA).

Philipkoski, Kristen. "Genetic Testing Case Settled." Wired News. April 10, 2001. Retrieved December 13, 2006 (http://www.wired.com/news/technology/0,1282,42971,00.html).

Wright, Robert. "James Watson & Francis Crick." Time.com. March 29, 1999. Retrieved December 13, 2006 (http://www.time.com/time/time100/scientist/profile/watsoncrick.html).

Index

Index

ABOUT THE AUTHOR

Elizabeth Boskey, Ph.D., M.P.H., is an assistant professor of preventive medicine and community health at SUNY Downstate Medical School, where she has lectured on genetic epidemiology. As a former researcher in maternal and child health, she has been interested in the ethical and practical issues surrounding genetic testing for many years. She is a certified health education specialist and has written or contributed to several books in the InVision Guide series from HarperCollins.

PHOTO CREDITS

Cover (left), p. 38 © Raveendran/AFP/Getty Images; cover (right) © Justin Sullivan/Getty Images; p. 5 © Stephen J. Carrera/AP/ Wide World Photos; p. 7 © www.istockphoto.com/Andrei Tchernov; pp. 10, 24, 44, 50 shutterstock.com; p. 14 © Dept. of Clinical Cytogenetics, Addenbrookes Hospital/Science Photo Library/Photo Researchers, Inc.; pp. 16, 17 © Hulton Archive/ Getty Images; p. 19 © Acey Harper/Time-Life Pictures/Getty Images; p. 21 © www.istockphoto.com/Marcin Balcerzak; p. 27 © Ross Setford/Getty Images; p. 29 © Yvonne Hemsey/Getty Images; p. 33 © Matt Cardy/Getty Images; p. 35 © Tim Boyle/ Getty Images; p. 36 © Keystone/Getty Images; p. 41 © Justin Sullivan/Getty Images; p. 46 Naval Research Laboratory.

Designer: Gene Mollica; **Editor:** Leigh Ann Cobb
Photo Researcher: Amy Feinberg